Louisiana Bingo Book

COMPLETE BINGO GAME IN A BOOK

UNION JUSTICE CONFIDENCE

Written By Rebecca Stark

ISBN 978-0-87386-511-1

Educational Books 'n' Bingo

Printed in the U.S.A.

DIRECTIONS

INCLUDED:

List of Terms

Templates for Additional Terms and Clues

2 Clues per Term

30 Unique Bingo Cards

Markers

1. **Either cut apart the book or make copies of ALL the sheets. You might want to make an extra copy of the clue sheets to use for introduction and review. Keep the sheets in an envelope for easy reuse.**

2. Cut apart the call cards with terms and clues.

3. Pass out one bingo card per student. There are enough for a class of 30.

4. Pass out markers. You may cut apart the markers included in this book or use any other small items of your choice.

5. Decide whether or not you will require the entire card to be filled. Requiring the entire card to be filled provides a better review. However, if you have a short time to fill, you may prefer to have them do the just the border or some other format. Tell the class before you begin what is required.

6. There are 50 terms. Read the list before you begin. If there are any terms that have not been covered in class, you may want to read to the students the term and clues before you begin.

7. There is a blank space in the middle of each card. You can instruct the students to use it as a free space or you can write in answers to cover terms not included. Of course, in this case you would create your own clues. (Templates provided.)

8. Shuffle the cards and place them in a pile. Two or three clues are provided for each term. If you plan to play the game with the same group more than once, you might want to choose a different clue for each game. If not, you may choose to use more than one clue.

9. Be sure to keep the cards you have used for the present game in a separate pile. When a student calls, "Bingo," he or she will have to verify that the correct answers are on his or her card AND that the markers were placed in response to the proper questions. Pull out the cards that are on the student's card keeping them in the order they were used in the game. Read each clue as it was given and ask the student to identify the correct answer from his or her card.

10. If the student has the correct answers on the card AND has shown that they were marked in response to the *correct questions,* then that student is the winner and the game is over. If the student does not have the correct answers on the card OR he or she marked the answers in response to *the wrong questions,* then the game continues until there is a proper winner.

11. If you want to play again, reshuffle the cards and begin again.

Have fun!

© Barbara M. Peller

TERMS INCLUDED

Agricultural

Battle of New Orleans

Baton Rouge

Bayou(s)

Beignet(s)

Border(s)

Cajuns

Civil War

William C.C. Claiborne

Climate

Confederate States of America

Crawfish

Creole(s)

Jefferson Davis

Robert de la Salle
  (René-Robert Cavelier, Sieur de La Salle)

Delta

East Gulf Coastal Plain

Estuary

Executive Branch

Fishing

Flag

Hurricane(s)

Industry (-ies)

Jazz

Judicial Branch

Lake(s)

Legislative Branch

Lowest Point

Louisiana Purchase

Mardi Gras

Mississippi Alluvial Plain

Mississippi River

Ernest Morial

Motto

Napoleon

Natchitoches

New Orleans

Parishes

Pelican

Pinckney's Treaty

Plantation(s)

River(s)

Shreveport

Song(s)

State

Steamboats

Streetcar(s)

Superdome

Treaty of Paris of 1763

West Gulf Coastal Plain

Additional Terms

Choose as many additional terms as you would like and write them in the squares. Repeat each as desired.
Cut out the squares and randomly distribute them to the class.
Instruct the students to place their square on the center space of their card.

Louisiana Bingo

Clues for Additional Terms

Write three clues for each of your additional terms.

1. _____ 2. 3.	1. _____ 2. 3.
1. _____ 2. 3.	1. _____ 2. 3.
1. _____ 2. 3.	1. _____ 2. 3.

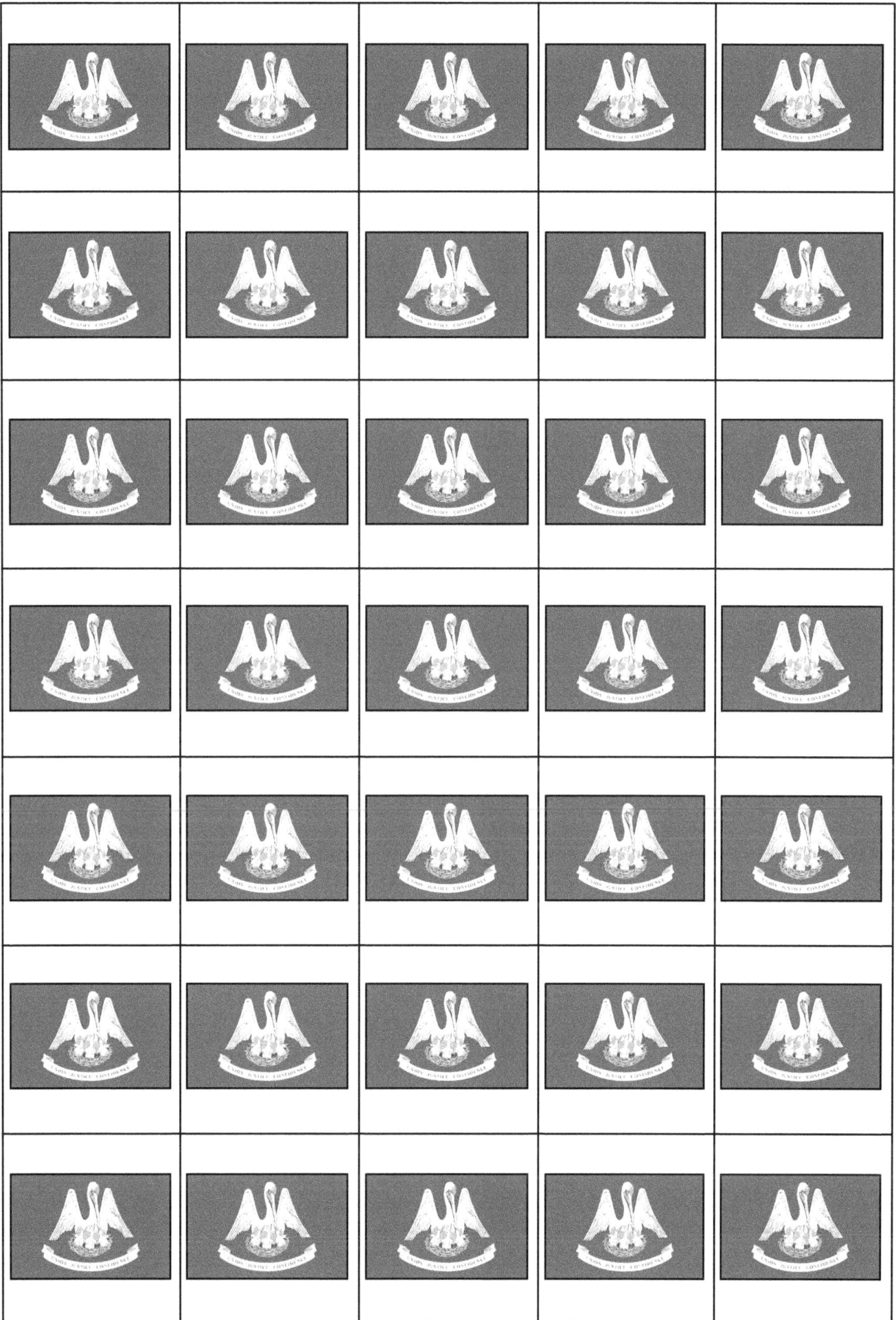

Agricultural 1. Sugar cane is the leading ___ product in the state. 2. The most important ___ products in terms of income generated are cane for sugar, rice, cattle and calves, soybeans, and cotton.	**Battle of New Orleans** 1. The ___ was the final major battle of the War of 1812. The Treaty of Ghent had been already been signed when the battle took place. 2. American forces, commanded by Major General Andrew Jackson, defeated an invading British Army at the ___.
Baton Rouge 1. ___ is the capital of Louisiana but not the largest city. 2. ___ is the second largest city in the state. It is a major industrial, petrochemical, medical, and research center.	**Bayou(s)** 1. The slow-moving, sometimes stagnant, outlets of Louisiana's lakes and rivers are called ___. 2. __ are commonly found in the Mississippi River region of the Gulf Coast. They provide a natural drainage system for rivers.
Beignet(s) 1. The ___ is the state doughnut. ___ are square, French-style doughnuts, covered with powdered sugar. 2. One of the most famous places to get ___ is the Café Du Monde in the New Orleans French Market. It opened in 1862.	**Border(s)** 1. Louisiana's ___ include Arkansas on the north, Mississippi on the east, and Texas on the west. 2. The Gulf of Mexico is the southern ___ of Louisiana.
Cajuns 1. ___ refers to people in southern Louisiana who are descendants of French colonists exiled from Acadia in the 18th century. 2. ___ is the style of cooking named for the French-speaking Acadian immigrants.	**Civil War** 1. Louisiana fought on the side of the Confederacy during the ___. 2. P.G.T. Beauregard and Richard Taylor were Confederate generals during the ___. They were both born in Louisiana.
William C.C. Claiborne 1. ___ was the first governor of Louisiana after it became a state. 2. ___ oversaw the transfer of Louisiana to U.S. control after the Louisiana Purchase in 1803. He governed when Louisiana was both a territory and a state. Louisiana Bingo	**Climate** 1. Louisiana has a semitropical ___, with long, hot, humid summers and short, mild winters. 2. Those parts of the state that are near the Gulf of Mexico tend to have a more humid ___ with little difference between the summer and winter. © Barbara M. Peller

Confederate States of America 1. The ___ was a government set up from 1861 to 1865. 2. Seven states, including Louisiana, seceded from the Union and formed the ___. Four other states later joined.	**Crawfish** 1. ___ is the state crustacean. 2. South Louisiana is called the ___ Capital of the World. In Louisiana, two species of ___ are harvested: the red swamp and the white river.
Creole(s) 1. ___ are descendants of the colonial settlers in Louisiana, especially those of French and Spanish descent. 2. The term ___ was first used during colonial times by the settlers to refer to those who were born in the colony.	**Jefferson Davis** 1. ___ was President of the Confederacy. 2. A parish is named for this Confederate President. Jennings is the parish seat.
Robert de la Salle **(René-Robert Cavelier, Sieur de La Salle)** 1. This French explorer was sent by King Louis XIV to travel south from Canada and sail down the Mississippi River to the Gulf of Mexico. 2. This French explorer named the Mississippi basin La Louisiane in honor of Louis XIV and claimed the region for France.	**Delta** 1. The Mississippi ___ at the mouth of the Mississippi River covers about 13,000 square miles. That is about 1/4 of the state. 2. The Mississippi ___ is the most fertile area of Louisiana.
East Gulf Coastal Plain 1. The ___ is the region east of the Mississippi River and north of Lake Pontchartrain. 2. This lowland region is east of the Mississippi. Near the river is marshland, but the land rises slightly in the north, where there are rolling hills.	**Estuary** 1. An ___ is a partly enclosed coastal body of water with one or more rivers or streams flowing into it. It has a free connection to the open sea. 2. Lake Pontchartain is actually an ___. It is connected to the Gulf of Mexico by way of the Rigolets.
Executive Branch 1. The governor is head of the ___. The present-day governor is [fill in]. 2. The ___ of government enforces laws. It comprises the governor, lieutenant governor, secretary of state, attorney general, treasurer, and various commissioners and agencies.	**Fishing** 1. Commercial ___, especially shellfish, is an important industry in Louisiana. 2. Important products of the commercial ___ industry include shrimp, oysters, catfish, crayfish, and menhaden.

Louisiana Bingo

Flag 1. A pelican feeding her young is displayed on a field of blue on the state ___. The state seal also features a pelican tending her young. 2. A ribbon with the state motto—"Union, Justice, and Confidence"—is on the state ___.	**Hurricane(s)** 1. ___ are severe tropical storms that form over warm ocean waters. The ___ season in Louisiana is from June 1 to November 30. 2. Louisiana is prone to ___. One of the most severe ___ to hit Louisiana was Katrina in 2005.
Industry (-ies) 1. Mining is an important ___. Petroleum and natural gas account for most of the state's mining income. 2. The production of chemicals and the processing of petroleum are important ___.	**Jazz** 1. Most agree that this type of music originated in New Orleans. 2. The Preservation Hall is a musical venue in the French Quarter founded in 1961 to protect and honor New Orleans ___.
Judicial Branch 1. The ___ is responsible for administering the laws of the state and resolving legal conflicts. 2. The ___ comprises a Supreme Court, courts of appeal, district courts, and other courts. The Supreme Court is the highest.	**Lake(s)** 1. Pontchartrain, Borgne, Maurepas, and Toledo Bend are ___ in the state. 2. Pontchartain is the considered the largest ___ in the state although technically it is an estuary.
Legislative Branch 1. The ___ comprises the Louisiana Senate and the Louisiana House of Representatives. 2. The ___ makes the laws.	**Lowest Point** 1. The ___ in the state is in New Orleans at 8 feet below sea level! The highest point, Driskill Mountain, is only 535 feet above sea level. 2. Complete this analogy: Driskill Mountain : Highest Point :: New Orleans : ___
Louisiana Purchase 1. In 1803 President Jefferson more than doubled the size of the United States with ___. 2. The ___ of 1803 included the acquisition of Louisiana Territory west of the Mississippi River, including the city of New Orleans. Louisiana Bingo	***Mardi Gras*** 1. This Carnival celebration held annually in New Orleans is known throughout the world. 2. Literally the name of this celebration means "Fat Tuesday." © Barbara M. Peller

Mississippi Alluvial Plain	Mississippi River
1. The ___ extends along the Mississippi River from Arkansas in the north to the Gulf of Mexico in the south. 2. This geographic region, which stretches along the Mississippi River, is characterized by ridges and hollows. Fields on the ridges are called the "frontlands."	1. The ___ is the principal river of the largest river system in North America. 2. The state's location at the mouth of the ___ has played an important role in the Louisiana's development.
Ernest Morial	**Motto**
1. This leading civil rights leader was the first black mayor of New Orleans. 2. New Orleans renamed its convention center, which spans over 10 blocks, after this late mayor.	1. The Louisiana ___ is "Union, Justice, and Confidence." 2. On the state flag is a ribbon with the state ___.
Napoleon	**Natchitoches**
1. ___ gained Louisiana Territory for France from Spain in 1800 under the Treaty of San Ildefonso. 2. In 1803 France, represented by ___, sold 828,000 square miles of land west of the Mississippi River to the United States of America.	1. ___ was the first permanent European settlement in the territory later known as the Louisiana Purchase. 2. Fort St. Jean Baptiste was built at ___ to prevent Spanish forces from the province of Texas from crossing the border into French Louisiane.
New Orleans	**Parishes**
1. This major port is the largest city in Louisiana. 2. The *Vieux Carré,* or French Quarter, is the oldest neighborhood in the city of ___. This district is a National Historic Landmark.	1. Louisiana is divided into 64 ___. 2. Louisiana is divided into ___. Alaska is divided into boroughs. The other 48 states are divided into counties.
Pelican	**Pinckney's Treaty**
1. The nickname for Louisiana is the ___ State. 2. The ___ is the state bird.	1. The Treaty of San Lorenzo of 1795, known as ___ , resolved territorial disputes between the Spain and the United States. 2. ___ granted American ships the right to free navigation of the Mississippi River and duty-free transport through the port of New Orleans. At that time the southern part of the Mississippi River was under Spanish control.

Louisiana Bingo

Plantation(s)	River(s)
1. A ___ is a large farm or estate on which cotton, tobacco, coffee, sugar cane, or other crop is cultivated. 2. Oakland, Oak Alley, Melrose, and Longue Vue are some antebellum Louisiana ___ that are now National Historic Landmarks. (antebellum = before the Civil War)	1. The Mississippi, Boeuf, Red, Ouachita, Atchafalaya, Sabine, and Pearl are ___ in Louisiana. 2. Levees have been built along the ___ to control flooding. They away some of the high water when it threatens to overspill the banks.
Shreveport 1. ___ is the third largest city in Louisiana. 2. ___ is the commercial and cultural center of the region known as Ark-La-Tex, the area where Arkansas, Louisiana, and Texas meet.	**Song(s)** 1. Louisiana has two official state ___, one official state environmental ___, and one official state march. 2. The best known of Louisiana's four state ___ is "You Are My Sunshine." It was written by former governor and country-music singer Jimmie H. Davis and Charles Mitchell.
State 1. James Madison was President when Louisiana became a ___ in 1812. 2. Louisiana was the first ___ west of the Mississippi River. It was the 18th ___ in the Union.	**Steamboats** 1. ___ are boats that are driven by steam power. They are used on rivers and other inland waterways. 2. Throughout the 19th century and the early 20th century, trade on the Mississippi River was dominated by paddle-wheel ___.
Streetcar(s) 1. The St. Charles Avenue ___ Line of New Orleans is the oldest continuously operating system of its type in the world. 2. ___ in New Orleans have been an integral part of the city's public transportation network since the first half of the 19th century.	**Superdome** 1. The ___ is a sports and exhibition arena located in the Central Business District of New Orleans. 2. It is one of the largest domed structures in the world. The Sugar Bowl is played here.
Treaty of Paris of 1763 1. The ___ ended the French and Indian War. 2. The terms of the ___ gave Britain the Spanish territories of East and West Florida.	**West Gulf Coastal Plain** 1. The ___ geographic region lies west of the Mississippi Alluvial Plain. 2. From south to north, the ___ region features beaches, marshland, and prairies. The highest point in the state, Driskill Mountain, is in this geographic region. It is about 40 miles from the Arkansas border.

Louisiana Bingo

Louisiana Bingo

Parishes	Agricultural	Baton Rouge	Executive Branch	Beignet(s)
East Gulf Coastal Plain	Battle of New Orleans	Superdome	*Mardi Gras*	Plantation(s)
Streetcar(s)	Louisiana Purchase		Napoleon	Treaty of Paris of 1763
Steamboats	Pinckney's Treaty	State	Lowest Point	Mississippi River
Motto	Hurricane(s)	Jefferson Davis	Song(s)	Judicial Branch

Louisiana Bingo

Steamboats	Streetcar(s)	Jazz	Pelican	Legislative Branch
Mississippi River	Robert de la Salle	Civil War	Pinckney's Treaty	Ernest Morial
Climate	Hurricane(s)		Industry (-ies)	State
Natchitoches	New Orleans	Louisiana Purchase	West Gulf Coastal Plain	Beignet(s)
Plantation(s)	Superdome	Jefferson Davis	East Gulf Coastal Plain	Song(s)

Louisiana Bingo

Hurricane(s)	State	Robert de la Salle	Lowest Point	Streetcar(s)
Mississippi River	Battle of New Orleans	William C.C. Claiborne	Agricultural	Flag
Pinckney's Treaty	Superdome		Ernest Morial	Bayou(s)
Louisiana Purchase	Climate	Motto	Natchitoches	Jazz
Song(s)	Confederate States of America	Jefferson Davis	West Gulf Coastal Plain	Legislative Branch

Louisiana Bingo

Louisiana Purchase	Ernest Morial	Baton Rouge	Confederate States of America	Legislative Branch
Mississippi Alluvial Plain	Cajuns	Agricultural	Pelican	Streetcar(s)
Napoleon	Natchitoches		Judicial Branch	Executive Branch
State	Battle of New Orleans	Superdome	Jefferson Davis	Civil War
Crawfish	Plantation(s)	Border(s)	Song(s)	Treaty of Paris of 1763

Louisiana Bingo

Plantation(s)	Beignet(s)	Pinckney's Treaty	Civil War	Confederate States of America
Mississippi Alluvial Plain	State	William C.C. Claiborne	Industry (-ies)	Battle of New Orleans
Baton Rouge	Treaty of Paris of 1763		*Mardi Gras*	Fishing
Judicial Branch	Legislative Branch	Parishes	West Gulf Coastal Plain	Creole(s)
Robert de la Salle	Jefferson Davis	Streetcar(s)	Louisiana Purchase	Napoleon

Louisiana Bingo: Card No. 5

Louisiana Bingo

Bayou(s)	Ernest Morial	Jazz	Legislative Branch	Treaty of Paris of 1763
Lowest Point	Pinckney's Treaty	Creole(s)	Agricultural	Streetcar(s)
Pelican	Crawfish		Cajuns	Industry (-ies)
Jefferson Davis	Motto	West Gulf Coastal Plain	Border(s)	Baton Rouge
Mississippi River	Civil War	Parishes	Napoleon	Delta

Louisiana Bingo

Parishes	Ernest Morial	Fishing	State	Robert de la Salle
Mississippi River	Legislative Branch	Hurricane(s)	Battle of New Orleans	Mississippi Alluvial Plain
Treaty of Paris of 1763	Executive Branch		Industry (-ies)	Cajuns
Louisiana Purchase	Natchitoches	William C.C. Claiborne	Steamboats	Climate
Jefferson Davis	Confederate States of America	West Gulf Coastal Plain	Border(s)	Bayou(s)

Louisiana Bingo: Card No. 7

Louisiana Bingo

Napoleon	Ernest Morial	Estuary	Lowest Point	Cajuns
Mississippi Alluvial Plain	Baton Rouge	Pelican	Treaty of Paris of 1763	Civil War
Delta	Confederate States of America		Legislative Branch	Beignet(s)
Song(s)	Louisiana Purchase	Steamboats	Crawfish	Natchitoches
Superdome	Jefferson Davis	Border(s)	Pinckney's Treaty	Mississippi River

Louisiana Bingo: Card No. 8

Louisiana Bingo

Industry (-ies)	Robert de la Salle	Hurricane(s)	Delta	Confederate States of America
Crawfish	Legislative Branch	Napoleon	Pinckney's Treaty	Ernest Morial
Flag	Parishes		Battle of New Orleans	Estuary
Creole(s)	Beignet(s)	Motto	*Mardi Gras*	Fishing
Natchitoches	West Gulf Coastal Plain	William C.C. Claiborne	Steamboats	Judicial Branch

Louisiana Bingo

Steamboats	Lowest Point	Cajuns	Pelican	Delta
Treaty of Paris of 1763	Civil War	Agricultural	Battle of New Orleans	Legislative Branch
Confederate States of America	Ernest Morial		Executive Branch	Climate
Motto	Judicial Branch	Creole(s)	West Gulf Coastal Plain	Flag
William C.C. Claiborne	Mississippi River	Jazz	Plantation(s)	Napoleon

Louisiana Bingo: Card No. 10

Louisiana Bingo

Bayou(s)	Ernest Morial	Pinckney's Treaty	Creole(s)	Mississippi River
Estuary	Flag	*Mardi Gras*	Industry (-ies)	Agricultural
Mississippi Alluvial Plain	Legislative Branch		Jazz	Hurricane(s)
William C.C. Claiborne	Streetcar(s)	West Gulf Coastal Plain	Confederate States of America	Steamboats
Crawfish	Jefferson Davis	Parishes	Border(s)	Robert de la Salle

Louisiana Bingo

Robert de la Salle	Beignet(s)	Flag	Lowest Point	Industry (-ies)
Hurricane(s)	Mississippi River	Baton Rouge	Border(s)	Battle of New Orleans
Parishes	Fishing		Treaty of Paris of 1763	Pelican
Jefferson Davis	Natchitoches	Legislative Branch	Steamboats	Mississippi Alluvial Plain
Ernest Morial	Estuary	Confederate States of America	Crawfish	Civil War

Louisiana Bingo: Card No. 12

Louisiana Bingo

Creole(s)	Beignet(s)	Bayou(s)	Flag	Treaty of Paris of 1763
Baton Rouge	Estuary	Legislative Branch	Industry (-ies)	Climate
Lowest Point	Civil War		Hurricane(s)	Fishing
Napoleon	West Gulf Coastal Plain	Cajuns	Confederate States of America	Steamboats
Jefferson Davis	Judicial Branch	Border(s)	Parishes	*Mardi Gras*

Louisiana Bingo: Card No. 13

Louisiana Bingo

East Gulf Coastal Plain	Legislative Branch	Pinckney's Treaty	Industry (-ies)	Crawfish
Civil War	Parishes	Flag	Battle of New Orleans	Ernest Morial
Creole(s)	Executive Branch		Jazz	William C.C. Claiborne
Judicial Branch	West Gulf Coastal Plain	Confederate States of America	Cajuns	Bayou(s)
Jefferson Davis	Pelican	Climate	Mississippi River	Napoleon

Louisiana Bingo

Mardi Gras	Industry (-ies)	Pinckney's Treaty	Robert de la Salle	Lowest Point
Bayou(s)	Jazz	Agricultural	Baton Rouge	Crawfish
Treaty of Paris of 1763	Parishes		Streetcar(s)	Ernest Morial
Jefferson Davis	Flag	Estuary	West Gulf Coastal Plain	Creole(s)
Mississippi River	Natchitoches	Border(s)	Delta	Hurricane(s)

Louisiana Bingo: Card No. 15

© Barbara M. Peller

Louisiana Bingo

Cajuns	Flag	Estuary	Delta	New Orleans
Pelican	Climate	Fishing	Mississippi Alluvial Plain	Executive Branch
Creole(s)	Beignet(s)		Treaty of Paris of 1763	Hurricane(s)
Louisiana Purchase	Civil War	Jefferson Davis	*Mardi Gras*	Steamboats
Crawfish	Shreveport	Border(s)	Natchitoches	Ernest Morial

Louisiana Bingo

William C.C. Claiborne	River(s)	Lake(s)	Flag	East Gulf Coastal Plain
Mardi Gras	Crawfish	West Gulf Coastal Plain	Executive Branch	Fishing
Industry (-ies)	Napoleon		Shreveport	Estuary
Judicial Branch	Mississippi River	Steamboats	Pinckney's Treaty	Climate
Motto	Creole(s)	Robert de la Salle	Lowest Point	Beignet(s)

Louisiana Bingo

Delta	Confederate States of America	Civil War	Creole(s)	Pelican
Ernest Morial	William C.C. Claiborne	Motto	Treaty of Paris of 1763	Crawfish
Industry (-ies)	Climate		Lake(s)	Baton Rouge
Beignet(s)	Agricultural	West Gulf Coastal Plain	Steamboats	Jazz
Shreveport	Flag	Pinckney's Treaty	River(s)	Bayou(s)

Louisiana Bingo: Card No. 18

Louisiana Bingo

Treaty of Paris of 1763	Bayou(s)	Flag	Estuary	Steamboats
Mardi Gras	Lowest Point	Ernest Morial	Robert de la Salle	Executive Branch
River(s)	Confederate States of America		Battle of New Orleans	Streetcar(s)
Jazz	Shreveport	Motto	Natchitoches	Lake(s)
Baton Rouge	New Orleans	Mississippi River	Napoleon	Border(s)

Louisiana Bingo

East Gulf Coastal Plain	River(s)	Lowest Point	Flag	Border(s)
Civil War	Hurricane(s)	Mississippi Alluvial Plain	Motto	Pelican
Beignet(s)	Fishing		Louisiana Purchase	Agricultural
Plantation(s)	Superdome	Song(s)	Natchitoches	Shreveport
State	Napoleon	New Orleans	Steamboats	Lake(s)

Louisiana Bingo: Card No. 20

Louisiana Bingo

Mardi Gras	Bayou(s)	Mississippi Alluvial Plain	Flag	Plantation(s)
Beignet(s)	Lake(s)	Cajuns	Estuary	Parishes
Climate	Mississippi River		River(s)	Pinckney's Treaty
Motto	Robert de la Salle	Shreveport	Judicial Branch	Napoleon
Louisiana Purchase	New Orleans	Border(s)	William C.C. Claiborne	Natchitoches

Louisiana Bingo

Delta	Jazz	Lake(s)	Baton Rouge	Creole(s)
Pelican	Lowest Point	Streetcar(s)	Estuary	Battle of New Orleans
Civil War	Executive Branch		Parishes	Fishing
Shreveport	Judicial Branch	Natchitoches	Agricultural	Mississippi Alluvial Plain
New Orleans	William C.C. Claiborne	River(s)	Climate	Louisiana Purchase

Louisiana Bingo: Card No. 22

Louisiana Bingo

Cajuns	River(s)	Robert de la Salle	Baton Rouge	Border(s)
Bayou(s)	East Gulf Coastal Plain	Mississippi River	*Mardi Gras*	Agricultural
Jazz	Creole(s)		Song(s)	Parishes
Climate	New Orleans	Shreveport	William C.C. Claiborne	Natchitoches
Plantation(s)	Superdome	Napoleon	Motto	Lake(s)

Louisiana Bingo

Cajuns	Napoleon	East Gulf Coastal Plain	River(s)	Estuary
Lake(s)	Border(s)	Mississippi Alluvial Plain	Pelican	Parishes
Fishing	Delta		Creole(s)	Climate
Plantation(s)	Song(s)	Shreveport	William C.C. Claiborne	Beignet(s)
State	Louisiana Purchase	New Orleans	Lowest Point	Superdome

Louisiana Bingo: Card No. 24

Louisiana Bingo

Louisiana Purchase	Mississippi Alluvial Plain	River(s)	Pinckney's Treaty	Lake(s)
Agricultural	Beignet(s)	*Mardi Gras*	Cajuns	Battle of New Orleans
Judicial Branch	Estuary		Song(s)	Shreveport
Streetcar(s)	Plantation(s)	Superdome	New Orleans	Executive Branch
Border(s)	East Gulf Coastal Plain	Civil War	Crawfish	State

Louisiana Bingo

Lake(s)	River(s)	Jazz	Pelican	Delta
Motto	Lowest Point	Estuary	East Gulf Coastal Plain	Cajuns
Judicial Branch	Song(s)		Executive Branch	Louisiana Purchase
William C.C. Claiborne	Baton Rouge	Plantation(s)	New Orleans	Shreveport
Fishing	Crawfish	Pinckney's Treaty	Superdome	State

Louisiana Bingo

Jazz	Civil War	River(s)	East Gulf Coastal Plain	Hurricane(s)
Plantation(s)	Song(s)	*Mardi Gras*	Shreveport	Battle of New Orleans
West Gulf Coastal Plain	Superdome		New Orleans	Louisiana Purchase
Delta	Bayou(s)	Mississippi Alluvial Plain	State	Agricultural
Crawfish	Executive Branch	Lake(s)	Streetcar(s)	Fishing

Louisiana Bingo: Card No. 27

Louisiana Bingo

Jazz	East Gulf Coastal Plain	Streetcar(s)	River(s)	Cajuns
Hurricane(s)	Lake(s)	Song(s)	Pelican	Executive Branch
Superdome	Climate		Fishing	Motto
Steamboats	Delta	Mississippi River	New Orleans	Shreveport
Baton Rouge	Industry (-ies)	Crawfish	State	Plantation(s)

Louisiana Bingo

Confederate States of America	River(s)	Pelican	Industry (-ies)	Shreveport
Agricultural	East Gulf Coastal Plain	Jazz	Executive Branch	Battle of New Orleans
Judicial Branch	Creole(s)		Fishing	Mississippi Alluvial Plain
State	Bayou(s)	Baton Rouge	New Orleans	Song(s)
Plantation(s)	Treaty of Paris of 1763	Superdome	Lake(s)	Streetcar(s)

www.ingramcontent.com/pod-product-compliance
Lightning Source LLC
LaVergne TN
LVHW061338060426
835511LV00014B/1984